Our yes to God

Chiara Lubich

our yes to God

new city press, new york

*Published in the United States by New City Press
the Publishing House of the Focolare Movement, Inc.
206 Skillman Avenue, Brooklyn, N.Y. 11211
© 1981 by New City Press, Brooklyn, N.Y.
Translated from the original Italian edition
Il "si" dell'uomo a Dio
by Hugh J. Moran
Printed in the United States of America
Library of Congress Catalog Number: 81-82064
ISBN 0-911782-38-9*

*Scripture quotations, unless otherwise noted, are
from the Revised Standard Version of the Bible,
copyrighted 1946, 1952 © 1971, 1973. Special
permission granted to use "in this publication"
the you-your-yours form of personal pronoun in the
address to God. Quotations marked with an asterisk are
from the New American Bible © 1970, Confraternity
of Christian Doctrine, or the New International
Version of the Bible © 1974, New York International
Bible Society.*

Nihil Obstat:	Charles E. Diviney, P.A.
	Diocesan Censor
Imprimatur:	Francis J. Mugavero, D.D.
	Bishop of Brooklyn
Brooklyn, N.Y. June 10, 1981	

Contents

*Humanity's "Yes" to God in the
Old and New Testaments*   7

*God's Will in the Spirituality of the
Focolare Movement*   29

The Church's "Yes" to God (part one)   51

The Church's "Yes" to God (part two)   71

*God's Will in Alphonsus Liguori,
Doctor of the Church*   97

Notes   111

CHAPTER ONE

Humanity's "Yes" to God in the Old and New Testaments

The purpose of this book is to examine in depth one of the key points of the spirituality of the Focolare Movement: God's will. We will look at what the Bible says about it; we will reflect on what we have understood about it through the life of the Movement; and we will consult the statements and writings of some of the Church Fathers, a number of saints, the recent popes, and the Second Vatican Council. Let us begin by considering several fundamental passages in the Old and New Testaments.

THE ESSENTIAL RELATIONSHIP BETWEEN GOD AND EACH HUMAN BEING

In order to understand what the Scriptures reveal to us about God's will, we must first look at the type of relationship that existed between God and the human race in the Old Testament.

Since God created the human race, each person is a creature and, as such, is completely dependent upon God. This is the basic relationship, the first thing we should keep in mind. All that a human being is and does, he or she is and does as a creature.

In creating the human race, however, God made human beings different from other creatures; he made them, as we know, in his own "image and likeness" (Gen. 1:26). But what does this really mean? It means that each human being is capable of a direct, personal relationship with God, a relationship of knowledge, love, friendship, and communion. It means that God created human beings as persons he can relate to, whom he can address as "you." As the theologian Westermann says, "Man's very essence is seen in his being 'face to face' with God. The relationship with God is not something added to human nature, rather Man is created such that his human nature is understood within his relationship with God."[1]

This relationship with God is what makes us human. That is how we have been created.

AN EXISTENTIAL RELATIONSHIP WITH GOD

Since the essential characteristic of human nature lies in this relationship with God (inasmuch as being human consists in being God's image) then we must develop this relationship and live it out in our day-to-day lives if we wish to reach self-fulfillment. We have been created in this relationship with God; therefore, we can find fulfillment only within the context of this relationship.

Humanity's "Yes" to God 11

The deeper our rapport with God becomes and the more it is lived and enriched, the more we ourselves are fulfilled and happy. By adhering to what God wants from us, to his plan for us, and by conforming our will to his, we reach our fulfillment as human beings.

GOD'S "YES" TO THE HUMAN RACE

God's special concern for the human race did not end with its creation, but has continued down through the ages. We see this in the Old Testament where the question is posed: "What is Man?" The psalmist asks God: "What is Man that you are mindful of him, and the son of man that you care for him [literally: that you visit him]?" (Ps. 8:5). Man can be properly understood, therefore, only as someone whom God is mindful of, whom God lovingly visits. Again the psalmist asks: "O Lord, what is Man that you regard him [literally: that you know him], or the son of man that you think of him? Man is like a breath, his days are like a passing shadow" (Ps. 144:3-5).

Even though we are mere transitory beings, God cares for us, knows us, listens to us. Although we are destined to die we belong to God.

In the Bible, the human race as well as each individual person is always considered as belonging to God and dependent on him. There is no way for anyone to escape from the presence of God—from him each of us has come, and before him alone our ultimate destiny will be decided.

Some people seek the basis for human dignity in the spiritual side of human nature or in other human values. The Bible shows us, however, that human dignity is based on the fact that God cares for the human race and for each human being, and that in the course of human history he visits us, meets us, and redeems us. And it is precisely because of this encounter with God, that the human race has a future and can look forward to it with hope.

This, then, is God's side of the relationship, his "yes" to the human race. But what has been humanity's response?

Humanity's "No" to God

God's "yes" to the human race when he created it was a definitive "yes." Not even humanity's "no" could cause it to waver.

Genesis tells of God's love for the human race, of how he surrounds the first human beings with signs of his benevolence, and puts them in a delightful garden. Even the command not to eat "of the tree of the knowledge of good and evil," can be

Humanity's "Yes" to God 13

counted among these good gifts, for it is out of love that God warns them, "...in the day that you eat of it you shall die" (Gen. 2:17).

But Adam and Eve violate God's command. Instead of complying with his will and accepting the fact that they are creatures, they try to assert themselves and become like God, not only ignoring him but turning against him. In them, all humanity attempts to overstep its limits, and to claim privileges that belong to God alone.

Created to be in relationship with God, called to respond with its "yes" to God's "yes," humanity answers instead, from the very beginning, with a refusal, with sin, with a "no."

GOD'S JUDGMENT AND GOD'S MERCY

Naturally, God's reaction to sin can be nothing other than a judgment condemning it, because sin is a serious matter. However, God does not abandon the human race. He punishes humanity, but he also saves it and sustains it. He expels Adam and Eve from the garden, but leaves them the gift of life; he drives Cain from the fertile land, but marks his forehead with a sign of protection. He sends the flood, but saves one family to be the ancestors of a new humanity, and promises them the stability of the natural order.

Thus the grace of God is greater than judgment.

Humanity's "Yes" to God

Then God chooses Abraham, and in him the human race finally says its "yes" to God. "Now the Lord said to Abram, 'Go from your country and your kindred and your father's house to the land that I will show you. And I will make of you a great nation, and I will bless you'" (Gen. 12:1-2). And Abraham obeys: "So Abram went, as the Lord had told him" (Gen. 12:4).

In choosing Abraham God is not choosing the Israelites alone, for in Abraham God sees all peoples: "In you all the families of the earth shall be blessed" (Gen. 12:3).

God's Plan for Humanity

Humanity's acceptance of God's call ushers in a whole new era. Abraham is now guided by God. He no longer bases his life on his own ideas, but on God's will. And God's plan for him and for all humanity begins to unfold.

Abraham's acceptance means that he must follow God's commands. And God initiates him into an adventure that leaves him no respite and

Humanity's "Yes" to God 15

continually calls him to new and ever higher goals.

Genesis presents Abraham in all his greatness, but also in his weakness. Despite his limitations, however, his "yes" allows God to carry out his plans.

This experience makes it possible for Abraham—and therefore the whole human race—to begin an ascent to ever-more-noble religious, moral, spiritual, and social heights. In following God, Abraham will have a future he never dreamed of, because God has promised it to him and God is faithful to his word.

Thus God's entry into Abraham's life is like a new beginning for human history, and it directs all of history toward one end: the definitive coming of the kingdom of God through Jesus.

The God of Israel is first and foremost a personal God, as he reveals by his name, "I AM WHO I AM" (Ex. 3:14), and by his desire for a covenant with the human race throughout the Old Testament. He addresses himself personally to the Israelites and continues to address himself personally to every human being; and from all he demands an equally personal response.

On Mount Sinai God reveals his will to Moses in the Ten Commandments. God says that he himself took the initial step by rescuing the Hebrews from their slavery in Egypt; now he asks that they respond to his saving deed by observing his Law.

This revelation confirms Israel as God's chosen people and Israel celebrates it as a very great event.

In the first part of the Decalogue, we find the most important laws for the Israelite community—those concerning its relationship with God. In the second part, there is a summary of the fundamental human rights—the right to life, to a family, etc.—and the duties that correspond to these rights.

Therefore, the existence of the people of Israel as the community of God's people requires two essential dimensions: one "vertical," their relationship with Yahweh, their God; and the other "horizontal," their relationship with one another and with all their fellow human beings. This horizontal relationship now takes on new importance because it is commanded by God as part of one's relationship with him. Thus, in a very basic way, the Ten Commandments safeguard the true concept of what it means to be human.

True "Images of His Son"

Let us now move on to the New Testament. We have seen that God has created us in his image and likeness, and that therefore the way for us to become what we were meant to be, and to reach fulfillment as human beings, is to live according to his image and likeness.

In the New Testament, now that God has sent us his Son, Jesus—who is God, yes, but God made man—for us to be like God, to conform ourselves to his image, means to conform ourselves to Jesus, or as Paul would say, "to be conformed to the image of his Son" (Rom. 8:29). In the Son we reach our fulfillment as children of the Father, even to the point of perfect likeness with God in heaven.

DOING GOD'S WILL BRINGS US TO FULFILLMENT

From what has been said up to now, it is clear that carrying out God's will makes us free, makes us more and more our true selves. Obeying God and adhering to his will furthers our development as human beings, releases our creativity, and brings out our true personal identity.

Doing God's will, therefore, is not something unnecessary or artificial, or in conflict with being oneself. It is not a question of resigning ourselves to a more or less desirable fate. And it is still less a matter of forcing ourselves to undergo an unpleasant situation while thinking: "God has decreed it so. That is how it must be. It is inevitable."

Doing God's will is something altogether different: it is the best thing we could possibly desire for ourselves. It is what we have been created for.

By doing God's will we are helping ourselves and others to see his plan for each of us personally and to come to a fuller realization of his overall plan to bring all people to salvation and to the glory of heaven.

Jesus Manifests God's Will in Its Entirety

The Commandments of the Old Testament not only express God's will for us; they also express his love. He has given them to us for our good because he loves us. However, they do not express the whole of his will. His will is more complex, manifold—it goes far beyond the letter of the Law understood even in its fullest sense.

In the fullness of time Jesus came to manifest God's will in its entirety. He did this in a total way, through his teaching and through his life.

His behavior—especially his giving of himself on the cross, which shows us the meaning of the love he taught—has become the norm for Christian behavior, a norm which cannot be completely codified because it is life and because it is love.

For a Christian, to do God's will means first of all to "live like Jesus," that is, to live in a loving filial relationship with the Father which is expressed by doing his will completely.

JESUS COMES TO COMPLETE THE LAW

Among the Jewish people, particularly after the exile, many felt that to be as close as possible to what God wanted them to be, they had to know and observe all the precepts and restrictions of the Law to the letter. But often this observance was so scrupulous that they lost sight of the foundation of the Law itself, that is, the relationship of love that each person must have with God.

Jesus, like the prophets, speaks out against this deformation of the Law.

Jesus has no intention of nullifying Scripture because for him, too, it is all God's Word. However, he says he has come to "fulfill" it (Mt. 5:17).

Jesus tries to show through his actions how some precepts of the Law are to be interpreted. For example, he heals on the Sabbath—which appears to violate the Law—in order to explain that "the Sabbath was made for Man, not Man for the Sabbath" (Mk. 2:27). He means by this that there is no need for people to become entangled in a thousand subtle distinctions regarding the Sabbath observance, because God has given the obligation of the Sabbath out of love for Man. Thus he puts the Sabbath rest into its rightful perspective.

When questioned by some of the Pharisees and Scribes regarding "the tradition of the elders," and asked why his disciples do not observe this, Jesus reminds his questioners that they have subordinated God's will to their own tradition, and he reasserts the importance of God's Commandment: "Honor your father and your mother" (Ex. 20:12). For these Pharisees and Scribes asserted that if someone offered God the money he would have used to help his parents, he was no longer obliged to assist them (see Mt. 15:1-9).

In short, Jesus acts as one who has a direct and authentic knowledge of the will of God expressed in the Law. He thereby reveals that he is the true interpreter of the Law.

He interprets it most clearly in the Sermon on the Mount (Mt. 5:21-48). There he refers to several commandments and customs, goes to their roots, and recasts them in that new form and with that fullness toward which the Law itself had been directed. It is not enough to refrain from killing; you must avoid anger toward your brother. Besides not committing adultery, you must not even desire another woman. Not only must you not swear falsely, but you should not swear at all. Not "An eye for an eye and a tooth for a tooth," but "If anyone strikes you on the right cheek, turn to him the other also" (Mt. 4:38,39). Not "You shall love your neighbor and hate your enemy," but "Love your enemies and pray for those who persecute you" (Mt. 5:43,44).

Jesus wants to prevent the observance of God's commandments from being reduced to mere external acts; he wants our hearts to change: "There is nothing outside a man which by going into him can defile him; but the things which come out of a man are what defile him" (Mk. 7:15). What is essential, therefore, is a personal relationship with God. And this is confirmed by what Jesus says with regard to charitable acts and acts of worship: they must be done not in order to "be praised by men," but as an expression of love for God (Mt. 6:1-17).

God's will as presented by Jesus, therefore, does not abolish the Law, but reveals a deeper and fuller dimension of the Law.

JESUS TAKES THE PLACE OF THE LAW

But in the fullness of time, the Law is no longer sufficient to express God's will in its entirety. What, then, is the will of God manifested by Jesus?

Announcing that the kingdom of God is near, Jesus warns us that we must convert in order to enter it. To convert means to leave everything, to sell everything in order to possess God, in order to enter his kingdom. We need only recall the parables of the hidden treasure and of the precious pearl, in which a man sells all he owns in order to buy them (Mt. 13:44-46). The Christian must therefore love God more than father, mother, wife, husband, possessions—even more than life itself (Mt. 19:29; Lk. 14:26). Everything must be subordinated to God and be put aside for love of him—in a concrete way by some, in a spiritual way by all of us. Jesus invites each person to choose God in a total way.

He asks for more, therefore, than what the Law requires. Indeed, when he says, "Leave the dead to bury their own dead; but as for you, go and proclaim the kingdom of God" (Lk. 9:60), he seems to be going against the Law which commands: "Honor your father and your mother."

Jesus takes the place of the Law.

FOR CHRISTIANS, JESUS IS THE LAW

For Christians, Jesus is the Ideal to follow. And to follow Jesus means to accomplish the Father's will perfectly, as he does. Jesus himself sums it up in the commandment, "Love one another as I have loved you. There is no greater love than this: to lay down one's life for one's friends" (Jn. 15:12-13*).

Jesus does not merely speak about this love which is God's will for the new era; he lives it to the utmost. He is the first to have this total love for God and neighbor which he requires of others. His way of living, his doing God's will in giving his life for others, is the new law which we must all follow.

Toward Our Total Fulfillment: Our Divinization

But Jesus does not simply ask us to imitate him in accomplishing the Father's will; he offers us something greater, much greater. Having infused love into our hearts through the Holy Spirit (see Rom. 5:5), he can now make us sharers—as he says in his testament (Jn. 13-17)—in his own relationship with the Father, in the relationships that exist among the persons of the Trinity. And he wants this reality to spread into the relationships among people. In this lies the highest possible fulfillment—the "divinization"—of the individual human being and of humanity itself. As the Church Fathers say, God became man in order to make Man God.

For the Early Church Jesus Was the Law

The meaning of Jesus' words was more deeply grasped by the early Church after his death and resurrection, because of the example of his life.

For the early Church, and for Paul in particular, the Christian's new life has Christ as its reference point: he is the incarnation of God's will for the Christian. Paul writes, "Welcome one another, therefore, *as Christ has welcomed you*" (Rom. 15:7). "Walk in love, *as Christ loved us and gave himself up for us*" (Eph. 5:2). "Your attitude must be *that of Christ*" (Phil. 2:5*). Summing it up in a single phrase, he speaks of the "law of Christ" (Gal. 6:2), that is, Christ as the law of a Christian.

GOD HAS PLACED HIS LAW IN HUMAN HEARTS

In concentrating on the observance of the Law, there is a danger that one may come to regard the Commandments as external constraints, and consequently have a servile relationship with God and a legalistic approach to his Word. On the other hand, there is also the risk of becoming too self-confident and proud of one's ability to observe the precepts of the Law.

In the new order, however, the words of Jesus, written in human hearts, cannot be considered as something imposed from without. They cannot give rise to a servile relationship with God, nor can they be an occasion for boasting about oneself. God himself, through the Spirit, has poured love into our hearts, and "love is the fulfilling of the law" (Rom. 13:10). In this way, what God wants

Humanity's "Yes" to God

becomes what each person wants in the depths of his or her heart.

SEEKING TO KNOW GOD'S WILL

Whatever the situation, a Christian can always be sure that it is God's will to love. How to love in the particular circumstances of one's everyday life is something each person must discover. Each of us, therefore, must know how to seek out and discern God's will. Paul's advice in this regard is: "Do not conform yourselves to this age but be transformed...so that you may judge what is God's will" (Rom. 12:2*).

His will can be discovered moment by moment, by listening to the voice of the Spirit within us and being docile to it. Paul writes to the Galatians, "Walk by the Spirit" (5:16), by which he means: be "led by the Spirit" (5:18).

So we must sharpen our supernatural sensitivity, the evangelical "instinct" that the Spirit has given us, which can be developed only by putting it to use.

Paul holds that two things are necessary in order to obtain this greater sensitivity to the voice of the Spirit. The first is to be part of a Christian community and to progress in living the life of mutual love within the community: "This is my prayer: that your love [that is, your Christian love lived in the community] may abound more and more in knowledge and depth of insight so that you may be able to discern what is best" (Phil. 1:9-10*).

The second prerequisite is prayer, because the knowledge of God's will is also a gift: "We have not ceased to pray for you, asking that you may be filled with the knowledge of his will" (Col. 1:9).

THE COMMANDMENTS AND THE WILL OF GOD

Since each Christian has the law of the Spirit in his or her heart, we might wonder whether the Commandments are still useful as rules of conduct to help us carry out God's will.

They are useful, indeed, because the law of the Christian is love and love is difficult to codify. We know how easy it is to confuse our own opinions and desires with the voice of the Spirit within us, and how easy it is, as a consequence, to act in a purely subjective manner, following our own feelings and inclinations.

Given our human, earthly condition, love needs to be explained and guided by objective norms which make its practical application easier and serve as sure points of reference.

Seen in this light, the Commandments become an aid for loving God and neighbor. And we Christians, convinced of this, should seek to understand the purpose behind each norm, the reason for its existence, in order to conform ourselves to the loving intention of the One who formulated it. Thus the written Law becomes a precious means put at our disposal. It is not, however, the goal of our lives.

For God's will is not that we obey a code of ordinances, but that we love him and our fellow human beings; and in this lies the fulfillment of the Law.

CHAPTER TWO

God's Will in the Spirituality of the Focolare Movement

We must be truly thankful to God for the many insights he has given us with regard to this very important aspect of Christian life, particularly at the beginning of our Movement, when he made use of providential circumstances to enlighten us, and suggested simple and effective examples that helped us to understand and do his will.

So that this wealth of experience may become the patrimony of each member of the Movement, I think it is appropriate for us to look back at the early days of the Movement, for I am reminded of the words of Scripture: "Recall the former days... after you were enlightened..." (Heb. 10:32).

NOT THOSE WHO SAY, "LORD, LORD," BUT THOSE WHO DO THE FATHER'S WILL

We had chosen God, who had manifested himself for what he is: Love. And we asked ourselves, "How can we love God with all our heart, with all our soul, with all our strength?" Then we remembered the words of Scripture, "Not every one who says to me, 'Lord, Lord,' shall enter the kingdom of heaven, but he who does the will of my Father" (Mt. 7:21). So we understood that to love God with all our heart, all our soul, all our strength, we had to do his will with all our heart, all our soul, all our strength.

It was clear, therefore, that loving God was not a matter of experiencing some particular sentiment, but of doing his will. To do his will became the practical way of showing our love for him.

We realized that we possessed a great gift— our free will—and that nothing could be more reasonable for us human beings, children of God, than to freely put our freedom at the service of the One who had given it to us. Thus from that moment on, we resolved to do not our own will, but God's will.

We immediately sought to unite our will to his. Our only will now was to do his will. In this way we would be truly loving him.

The state of perfection vs. perfection

At about that same time—I do not remember whether before or after—an experience of mine helped us to understand something very important. In December of 1943, God had called me to consecrate myself to him with a vow of chastity. Then, during midnight Mass on Christmas of the same year, I felt in my heart that Jesus was asking me to give him *everything*. By "everything" I naturally understood what most people in my situation would have understood at that time: that in addition to the vow of chastity, I should give God my own will through the vow of obedience and all that could be considered mine through the vow of poverty, and that I should leave my family and the beautiful things of the world by entering a cloister—the strictest form of cloister. I said "yes" to God, although I wept and was in torment because of something rebelling within me.

The next day I went to my confessor, and since he knew of the life that was springing up around me—I had already been joined by my first companions—he said very decisively, "No. This is not God's will for you."

At that moment, two ideas which in my mind had previously coincided, became distinct: the so-called *state* of perfection, and perfection. I understood then that although undoubtedly there were states of life that were more or less perfect, *perfection* could be attained only by doing God's will.

A WAY TO HOLINESS FOR EVERYONE

I remember that until that moment I felt as if a high wall were blocking my way to holiness. And I had been trying to find a breach in that wall. I used to think: if it is a matter of doing penance, then we should wear hair shirts all day long and scourge ourselves till we bleed. Or if it is a matter of praying, we should pray all day long.... But the question still remained: "What must we do to become saints?" I simply did not know. It was principally through this experience I just mentioned, that God enlightened me, and I understood that to reach sanctity it is enough to do his will.

It was a wonderful discovery! And so practical too. Here was a way that was good for everyone: men and women, young and old, gifted and less gifted, intellectuals and laborers, mothers and those in religious life, lay people and clergy, government officials and ordinary citizens. Here was a way to sanctity wide-open to every human being. I felt I had in my hands the passport to perfection—not only for an elite group of persons called to the priesthood or religious life, but for the masses.

A DIVINE ADVENTURE

I saw that two roads lie before us in life, and that my friends and I, like everyone else, would have to choose between them: we could spend this life either following our own will, or following God's will.

If we followed our own will, our destiny would

God's Will in the Focolare Movement   35

be like that of almost everyone else in the world. Each day many people die, and the tears and flowers show that their death causes much suffering. But then, after another generation has passed, most of them have been forgotten.

If, instead, we walked the way of God's will, he would guide us moment by moment along paths conceived by his love, invented by his imagination, and suggested by his providence, which cares for each of us as individuals and for the community as a whole. He would lead us on a marvelous, divine adventure, as yet unknown to us. And our lives would not end in silence, but would remain to give light to many, like the lives of the saints.

We were so convinced that choosing God's will was the good, worthwhile, beautiful, beneficial thing to do, that we were struck by what we considered the strange way of reasoning of so many people who limit themselves to being resigned to God's will. We used to say: "What?... *Resign* ourselves to God's will? On the contrary! We should have to resign ourselves if we do our own dull will, so unprofitable and inconclusive!" We should *want* to do God's will because it is the greatest thing we could desire. And we should not say, "I *must* do God's will," but rather, "I *can* do God's will!"

Seen in this perspective, all our personal plans

fell into insignificance and we abandoned ourselves completely to God.

We knew that God's will was a Father's will. We could place ourselves in his hands without fear. Certainly, anything that he willed would be for our good.

We believed in love.

This complete trust in God did not mean we became passive. Quite the contrary: once we had grasped God's will, we made it our own and carried it out with all our heart, with all our soul, with all our strength, endeavoring to be as faithful to it as possible even though it was constantly changing.

When we did not know what God wanted, we did what we thought best, asking God to put us back on the right track if we had made the wrong choice.

Before long, we had acquired a considerable amount of the flexibility one must have in order to be able to understand his will.

We knew that by living this way we were putting into effect a divine plan, about which we knew nothing except that we were being guided by God, our Father, and that every circumstance was an expression of his love for us.

JESUS: OUR MODEL IN DOING THE FATHER'S WILL

Living like this, we were struck by many passages of Scripture. Jesus had said, "My food is to do the will of him who sent me" (Jn. 4:34), and we wanted to be able to say the same. He had also said, "I have come down from heaven, not to do my own will, but the will of him who sent me" (Jn. 6:38). "Nevertheless not my will, but yours, be done" (Lk. 22:42). "I always do what is pleasing to him" (Jn. 8:29). "I have come to do your will, O God" (Heb. 10:7).

Jesus was our example. We imitated him, not in an exterior way—as, for example, in his scourging or in going without a traveling bag—but in the fact that, like him, we wanted to do God's will. This is reflected in the following passage from a meditation I wrote in 1946.

> Each of us must aim at being another Jesus as soon as possible; we must act as Jesus here on earth....
>
> We must put our human nature at God's disposal so that he can use it to make his beloved Son live again in us.
>
> In order to do this we should do only God's will, as Jesus did.
>
> May we always be able to have on our lips the words Jesus used in reference to himself....

When we have succeeded in being able to be like Christ in his determined, total obedience to the Father, then we will experience inner unity.

IMITATING THE SAINTS

We viewed the saints from the same perspective. We were not to imitate them by mindlessly copying their actions, but by striving to do God's will as they had done.

How different they all were from one another; yet they were identical in one thing: they all had done God's will.

At that time our whole purpose in life was summed up in doing God's will. For example, being consecrated to God with vows was something important, but God's will was more important.

I remember that I considered my sister who was called to married life to be just as fortunate as I. I felt we were truly equal. I said to her: "You are getting married, and you are doing God's will. I will live a life of virginity. But we are equal because what is important is God's will."

To do God's will was the norm that bound us together as one family with Jesus our brother and God our Father.

Understanding God's Will: The "New Commandment"

We found God's will expressed for us above all in the new spirituality that was coming to life. We had chosen to live for God alone, and had understood that in order to be faithful to this choice, we had to put into practice the commandment that Jesus calls his own: the "new commandment" (Jn. 13:34; 15:12).

This commandment influenced everything we did. To carry it out as well as possible, we made a pact. And we recognized that even our love for Jesus forsaken—that is, for Jesus in the moment of his greatest suffering when he cried out, "My God, my God, why have you forsaken me?" (Mt. 27:46)—was an integral part of being faithful to this commandment. Moreover, it was living this command that brought about the unity willed by Jesus and enabled us to have him present in our midst. And the desire to live this command well gave us added incentive to live all the other words of the Gospel.

God had focused our attention on the new commandment, and now we realize more and more that in so doing he had revealed to us the very heart of Christianity.

OTHER EXPRESSIONS OF GOD'S WILL

God's will was also manifested to us by the Ten Commandments, as well as by the precepts of the Church, by our superiors, and by the duties of our state in life. Even civil laws were an expression of God's will for us, as were life's various circumstances, whether they were joyful, sorrowful, or indifferent.

LISTEN TO "THAT VOICE"[1]

We had a kind of compass for determining God's will. It was the "voice" within us, the voice of the Holy Spirit. We used to urge one another to listen to "that voice." At that time, for us to speak of a "voice" meant to risk being taken for heretics. And it was equally difficult for us as lay people to speak about the Gospel or about love.

We got used to listening to "that voice" in order to know God's will. Later on, in the light of this experience, we understood that one of the reasons why God had created the Focolare was that the presence of Jesus in our midst in the Focolare was like a loud-speaker that amplified God's voice within each one of us, enabling us to hear it more clearly. We often say that in the Focolare we live between two "fires": God within us and God in our midst. Here in this divine

God's Will in the Focolare Movement 41

"furnace" we are formed and trained to listen to Jesus and to follow him. We are encouraged by the fact that St. Paul himself is clearly of the opinion that in order to understand God's will, a person should be part of a Christian community where Christ is alive and present (see Phil. 1:9-10).

THE PRESENT MOMENT

At the beginning of the Movement we were in constant danger of losing our lives, because we were not adequately sheltered during the air raids. So when the question arose as to when we had to do God's will in order to love him, we immediately understood that the answer was: now—right now. For we did not know if we would still be alive later.

The only time in our possession was the present moment. The past was already gone, and we did not know if the future would ever come. We used to say: "The past no longer exists; let's entrust it to God's mercy. The future is not yet here. By living the present, we will also live the future well when it becomes the present."

We realized how foolish it was to live in the past, which will never return, or in the future, which may never come and which, in any case, is unpredictable.

We took the example of riding on a train. Just as a traveler remains seated and would not think of walking up and down the aisle in order to get to the destination sooner, so we had to remain in the present. The train of time moves ahead on its own.

Living the present, one moment after another, we will one day reach that decisive moment upon which our eternity depends. Having loved God's will in the present with all our heart, all our soul, all our strength, we will have fulfilled, throughout our lives, the commandment to love God with all our heart, all our soul, all our strength.

THE EXPRESSED AND UNFORESEEN ASPECTS OF GOD'S WILL

Employing a distinction used at the time, we noted the difference between the divine will already "signified" for us and the divine will of God's "good pleasure" not yet manifested to us, in other words, between what we might call God's "expressed" will and his "unforeseen" will. God's expressed will included all that we *knew* we had to abide by: the Commandments, the Word of God, the precepts of the Church, the duties of our state in life, etc. God's "good pleasure," on the other hand, referred to the various unforeseen aspects of his will which are made manifest to us through events and circumstances, such as an unexpected encounter, a fortunate occurrence, a tragedy, a new situation, etc.

We tried to carry out the expressed will of God

God's Will in the Focolare Movement   43

as perfectly as possible, while maintaining the flexibility necessary in order to be able to change our course of action as soon as circumstances revealed that God wanted something different from us.

Among the first members of the Movement some were inclined to be more attentive to one or the other of these expressions of God's will. We noted the positive and negative aspects of both attitudes, and we concluded that perfection consisted in being able to grasp what God wanted in the present moment, and doing it.

Those who were more inclined to carry out the expressed will of God, and less concerned with the unforeseen aspects of his will, tended not to notice when circumstances indicated a new course of God's will, and consequently they tended to have a less intimate relationship with him, not giving themselves to him with all their heart. So although they believed they were devoted to their duties, they were, in fact, devoted to themselves!

On the other hand, those who were more inclined to do God's will as manifested by circumstances had a greater appreciation of the "poetry" of the Gospel, and found it easier to see the "golden thread" of God's providence running through everything that happened. At times, however, aided by their imagination, they thought they saw God everywhere; and they presented the life of the

Gospel in a way which was too adventurous and romantic. By so doing, they deprived the Gospel life of its most beautiful characteristic: the *normality* of a life that is supernatural, but simple; neither artificial nor excessive, but pure and harmonious—as nature is, as Mary is.

Consequently, we made a determined effort to become more and more adept at perceiving God's plan for each one of us in every present moment, and to truly *be* what he wanted of us, in each moment.

THE RAY OF GOD'S WILL

To illustrate how we wanted to live, we used the image of the sun with its rays. The sun was God, the rays his will. Each one of us, in each present moment of our life, had a ray of the sun to walk in, that is, God's will for him or her. Each person's ray was distinct from the others; yet all were rays of the sun, all were God's will. Therefore, all of us were doing only one will—God's will—but it was different for each person. Because of this one will—which bound us to one another, to Jesus, and to the Father—each one of us felt that he or she was one with each of the others, with Jesus, and with the Father.

As the rays of the sun are *one* with the sun,

God's Will in the Focolare Movement 45

similarly, God's will coincides with God. Thus, by loving his will, we were loving him.

We had to follow our ray: always walking in it, always being enlightened by it—remaining constantly in God's will. To do this successfully, we needed to use violence at times in order to silence our own will and to hold fast to his, which is, after all, the expression of his love for us.

When we succeeded in doing his divine will consistently in many successive present moments, we experienced that his yoke was light and easy (Mt. 11:29).

Everything in our lives changed. For example, our relationships with others: previously we used to associate with people we liked, and we loved those whom we found pleasant. But now we were happy to seek the company of whomever God willed us to be with, and we would stay with them for as long as he willed it.

The fact that we were completely intent upon doing God's will in each present moment led to our being detached from everything else, and from ourselves as well. This detachment was not something deliberately sought after—we sought God alone. It simply came as a consequence, because two things could not occupy our attention at the same time. Where there was the divine will, there was no room for ours. In the present moment we could not do two things at once. So rather than labor to eradicate our own will, we worked to acquire the divine will.

GETTING BACK IN OUR RAY

Whenever we realized that we had "gone out of our ray," as we used to say, into the darkness, and had spent a few moments doing our own will and letting our old self[2] live, we knew the only way to improve the situation was to start doing the divine will of that present moment. Since we had not loved God in those previous moments, we had to love him at least in that present moment.

We felt that with each passing moment of each new day, we were adding stitches to a magnificent embroidery. Those moments which we had not spent "in our ray" were entrusted to God's mercy. To us, looking from below—from the underside of the embroidery, as it were—those moments seemed like so many knots in the threads. But we knew that this was simply our human way of looking at things. We were certain that God's love mends every tear and binds every broken thread. And so we knew that, seen right side up—from God's vantage point—the design would turn out perfectly. And from heaven our lives would be seen as the wonderful stories of true children of God.

We liked very much something St. Francis de Sales had said about the relationship between Christians and God's will. It could be paraphrased in this manner: "True Christians will carry this name engraved in their hearts: 'I am God's will for me.'"[3]

ALL THAT GOD WILLS OR PERMITS IS FOR OUR GOOD

Everything that God asked of us was love. In each moment he came to us in his will; and whether this appeared beautiful or sad to us, it was nonetheless he himself coming to us with his love.

But how were we to consider the things he merely allowed to happen? What about our mistakes, our weaknesses? From the very beginning, Catherine of Siena was an encouragement to us in this regard, with her statement, "All that God wills or permits is for our sanctification."[4]

So we knew we should never let anything stop us. If we made a mistake, we could not let it get us down. Whatever happened, if entrusted to God's mercy, would not only cease to be useless or harmful, but would help us to acquire humility, which is the foundation for sanctity.

In fact, Scripture says, "God makes all things work together for the good of those who love him"

(Rom. 8:28). We had wanted to love God, and we discovered that, as a result, everything that happened in life would contribute to our personal spiritual growth.

As we strove to do God's will, the Holy Spirit soon taught us that it was good to do the good that God wanted, but it was bad to do the good that God did not want. This understanding made our new life even more dynamic.

Doing God's will with all our heart, with all our mind and with all our strength brought us great peace and deep joy—peace and joy that the world cannot give but that only God can bestow.

Outside of God's will we found no light, no love, no peace—only torment.

Thus we learned to distinguish between natural and supernatural life. Even before then we had possessed supernatural life and God's grace, but we had not done enough to make this divine life bear fruit. Even though we were baptized we practically lived like pagans, because our hearts and minds were attached to many things instead of to God alone.

A NEW UNDERSTANDING OF MARY

In living according to God's will we also came to a deeper understanding of Mary. We admired her as the most perfect creature who had ever lived on this earth, because she had done only God's will.

Therefore, if doing God's will meant "to live as Jesus," it also meant "to live like Mary": this was the best way to show our devotion to her and to be her children. We took as our own her words, "I am the servant of the Lord. Let it be done to me as you say" (Lk 1:38*).

GOD'S PLAN FOR US:
A NEW MOVEMENT IN THE CHURCH

But this effort to do God's will always, moment by moment, brought about another effect in our lives. Since in doing his will we were loving him, and he manifests himself to those who love him (Jn. 14:21), he manifested himself to us.

From the very beginning, and continuing down through the years to the present, the Holy Spirit has been gradually revealing to us the splendid plan God had for each one of us and for our group.

This divine plan has brought a new movement to life in the Church: a movement beautiful beyond words; sacred, like all that is both human and divine; alive, like the Body of Christ, of which it is an expression; and rich—infinitely rich—because it was designed in heaven. And urged on by its divine architect, the Movement is intent upon resolving—together with other Christian movements—the most significant problems facing humanity today.

The Church has studied the Movement, has blessed it and approved it, and has confirmed its life as being God's will for all who belong to it and all whom God will call to be part of it in the future.

CHAPTER THREE

The Church's "Yes" to God (part one)

Scripture makes it clear that we should do God's will. And the saints also exhort us to do so. For example, Maximilian Kolbe writes to his mother in these words:

> I will wish you, Mother, neither health nor prosperity. Why? Because I want to wish you better than that, something so good that God Himself would not wish you better: that in all things, the will of this very good Father be accomplished in you, Mother, that you may know in all things how to fulfill the will of God! This is the very best I can wish for you. God Himself could not wish better than that.[1]

Let us now compare our own experience, point by point, with what we find in the Church Fathers, the saints, the popes and the Second Vatican Council.

OUR WILL MUST COINCIDE WITH GOD'S WILL

The Lord made us understand that our will must coincide with his.

Francis de Sales says, "The soul that loves God is so transformed into the divine will that it merits, rather, to be called God's will than to be called obedient and subject to his will."[2] And a "precious grace" received by Catherine of Siena "was the conformity of her will with, and, as it were, the absorption of her will into, the will of God."[3] This transformation of Catherine's will was so perfect that she did not hesitate to write, even to the popes, "Thus you will do God's will and mine."[4]

SANCTITY AND GOD'S WILL

It was clear to us from the very beginning of the Movement that by doing God's will we could reach sanctity. The saints, too, say that perfection lies precisely in this.

Catherine of Siena, for instance, is convinced that whoever takes this road will travel swiftly from one virtue to the next. And she writes:

> *O tender, loving Jesus, may your will be accomplished in us always,* as it is in heaven *by your angels and saints.... Then the soul...will run like an unbridled horse, from grace to grace, at full speed, and from virtue to virtue. It will no longer have any restraints to hold it back from running because it will have cut away from its own will*

every disordinate appetite and desire, for these are reins and fetters that obstruct the race of spiritual persons.[5]

Teresa of Avila, whose way to reach God was prayer, is of the same opinion. She has no doubt that perfection lies in doing God's will, and that the more one does so, the more graces one receives.

> All that the beginner in prayer has to do—and you must not forget this, for it is very important—is to labor and be resolute...to bring his will into conformity with the will of God.... This comprises the very greatest perfection which can be attained. The more perfectly a person practices it, the more he will receive of the Lord and the greater the progress he will make on this road.[6]

This is how she corrects those who think that perfection is to be found in mystical phenomena:

> It will become quite clear that the highest perfection consists not in interior favors, or in great raptures, or in visions, or in the spirit of prophecy, but in the bringing of our wills into conformity with the will of God.[7]

And she gives a personal example:

> While I was wondering if the people were right who disapproved of my going out [to found mon-

56   OUR YES TO GOD

asteries] and if I should do better to occupy myself continually in prayer, I heard these words: "For as long as life lasts there is no gain to be had in striving to [enjoy Me more], but only in doing My will."[8]

For Paul of the Cross, "The highest perfection consists in being perfectly united to the Most Holy Will of God."[9] And Paul VI tells us what holiness is in these words:

> This holiness to which we are called, is the result of two component factors, the first of which...is the grace of the Holy Spirit.... To be in the grace of God is everything for us. Our perfection is the possession of divine charity. [But] is there nothing else to be done? Yes, another factor is necessary... if we do not wish to fall into quietism or moral indifference. It is our "yes"; it is making ourselves available for the Spirit, and accepting—even more, desiring—the will of God....[10]

John XXIII affirms that "real greatness lies in doing the will of God, entirely and perfectly."[11]

God's Divine Plan for Us

As for us, from the very beginning we have always believed that if we do God's will and not our

The Church's "Yes" to God

own, then our lives will be following the pattern of his divine plan.

Paul VI recalls the example of St. Joseph, who had such an extraordinary destiny because he was always faithful and constant in listening to the Almighty, and he comments:

> The splendid plans of God, the provident enterprises that the Lord has in mind for human destinies, can co-exist with and rise above the most ordinary conditions of life....
>
> To conform our capricious, obstinate, often mistaken, sometimes even rebellious will to his; to make this small but sublime will coincide...with the will of God...*is the secret to living a great life.* It is to merge ourselves with the Lord's thoughts and to enter the plans of his omniscience and mercy as well as of his immense generosity.[12]

RESIGNATION TO GOD'S WILL

We have already seen that in the early days of the Movement, the words "God's will be done" were definitely not an expression of mere resignation for us. To do God's will was our greatest joy, our greatest glory!

In his book, *The Way,* Josemaría Escrivá de Balaguer, founder of "Opus Dei" writes: "Resignation?...Conformity? *Love* the Will of God!"[13] And he sees four steps in the development of a Christian's spiritual life, which are, appropriately, "to be resigned to the Will of God; to conform to the Will of God; to want the Will of God; to love the Will of God."[14]

Likewise, for Paul of the Cross:

> It is great perfection to resign oneself in all things to the divine will; it is greater perfection to live with great indifference, abandoned to God's good pleasure; the greatest, highest perfection is to nourish oneself, in a pure spirit of faith and love, on the divine will.[15]

How to know God's will

As I described in the previous chapter, we wanted to know God's will and, from the start, we did our best to discover it. When we had doubts about what to do in the present moment, we would decide on a certain course of action, asking God at the same time to put us back on the right track if we had made the wrong choice.

John of the Cross has something beautiful to say in this regard. He suggests that spiritual persons can obtain light and guidance from two sources: "natural reason and the law and doctrine of the Gospel."[16]

Elizabeth of the Trinity reminds us that God's will is also contained in the Rule the Church has given us: "From morning to night, the Rule is there to express God's will for us moment by moment. If you only knew how I love this Rule which is the form in which he wants me to reach sanctity."[17]

JESUS: OUR MODEL IN DOING GOD'S WILL

From the very first days of this new life, the Holy Spirit made us see clearly that Jesus was the one who had perfectly accomplished God's will. This is confirmed by Paul VI:

> If the break in the life-giving relationship between God and mankind resulted from an act of rebellion on the part of man, eager for an independence that was to be fatal to him, with the cry: "I will not serve" (Jer. 2:20), reparation could only come through a contrary attitude, the one assumed by Jesus, the Savior, to whom, in the Letter to the Hebrews (10:5-7), the following words are attributed: "Coming into the world he said: '...Lo, I have come to do your will, O God...'" (cf. Ps. 40:7-9).[18]
>
> One cannot understand and reconstruct something of the figure of Christ without regarding the essential importance which fulfillment of the Father's will assumes in Him....[19]

If all that Jesus did was done in order to obey the Father, he is our model. Moreover, he acted in such a way that we can imitate his example. Augustine points this out:

> "Father," he said, "if it be possible, let this cup pass from me." This was the human will which wanted something of its own.... But...he added, "nevertheless, not as I will, Father, but as you will" (Mt. 26:39).... Therefore, that you might want something different from what God wants is permitted because of human frailty...it would be most unusual if you did not want some particular thing. But immediately reflect on the One who is above you. He is above you, you are below him; he is the Creator, you are the creature; he is the Lord, you are the servant.... That is why he corrects you, why he causes you to submit to the Father's will, saying on your behalf: "Nevertheless, not as I will, Father, but as you will."[20]

John of the Cross reflects upon our desire to know God's will and then, "comparing the age of the written Law of the Old Testament with the age of the law of the Gospel and of grace, he warns us against desiring to be advised of God's will through extraordinary revelations and oracles accompanied by visions and voices. Even though such ways of knowing God's will were legitimate under the Old Covenant, they are no longer legitimate now."[21]

The reason he gives for this conclusion is simply splendid!

> Now that the faith is established through Christ, and the Gospel law made manifest...there is no reason for inquiring of Him in this way, or expecting Him to answer as before. In giving us His Son...He spoke everything to us at once....[22]

Jesus, therefore, *is* the Father's entire message to us. In him, in his life, and in his teachings, we find what we must do. Writing in the third century, Cyprian put it this way:

> God's will is what Christ both did and taught: humility in behavior, firmness in faith, modesty in words, justice in deeds, mercy in works, uprightness in morals. It is to not even know what it means to do injury to another; it is to bear insults patiently, to maintain peace with the brethren, to love God with all one's heart, to love him as Father and to fear him as God. It is to put aside everything for Christ because he put aside everything for us, to remain inseparably united to his love, to stay close to his cross...and, when the time comes to fight for his name...to be steadfast and open in giving witness to him, confident in the midst of torture, and patient in accepting the death for which we will receive the crown. This...is what it means to accomplish the Father's will.[23]

THE SAINTS—ALL DIFFERENT, YET ALIKE IN ACCOMPLISHING GOD'S WILL

We observed that the saints were so different from one another that each seemed a masterpiece, a unique creation of God's imagination. Yet they were all alike in that each had accomplished God's will. We have countless examples to choose from, but let us take Therese of Lisieux. Doing God's will was the dominant theme in her life:

> I desire only His will.[24]
>
> *My God,* "I choose all!" *I don't want to be a saint by halves, I'm not afraid to suffer for You, I fear only one thing: to keep my own will; so take it, for* "I choose all" *that You will!*[25]

A few months before her death she declared:

> My heart is filled with God's will, and when someone pours something on it, this doesn't penetrate its interior; it's a nothing which glides off easily, just like oil which can't mix with water.[26]

One of those present during her last agony tells us that the prioress, Mother Marie de Gonzague, asked her: "'And if it were God's will to leave you on the cross for a long time, would you accept it?' With extraordinary heroism she said: 'I would.'"[27]

Because she had lived this way, at the end of her life she was able to make the extraordinary statement: "In heaven the good God will do all I wish, because I have never done my own will upon earth."[28]

WHERE WE FIND GOD'S WILL EXPRESSED

Let us now consider where, and by whom, we find God's will expressed. We have repeatedly seen that, first of all, we find God's will in Jesus: he is *the* model of Christian behavior. Furthermore, he is also the revelation of God's will for all humanity: he tells us what God wants from us as human beings.

The Second Vatican Council reminds us that "'God our Savior...wishes [and, thus, Jesus wishes] all men to be saved and to come to the knowledge of the truth' (1 Tim. 2:3-4)."[29]

The Council further declares that all human beings are called to be one people and that this is likewise God's will.

> All men are called to belong to the new People of God. Wherefore this People, while remaining one and unique, is to be spread throughout the whole world and must exist in all ages, so that the purpose of God's will may be fulfilled. In the beginning God made human nature one. After His

children were scattered, He decreed that they should at length be unified again (cf. Jn. 11:52).[30]

Another aspect of God's will expressed in the Gospel is that we should see and love Jesus in all persons. The Last Judgment will be based on this point. The Council clearly affirms: "The Father wills that in all persons we recognize Christ our brother and love Him effectively in word and in deed."[31]

God also wants the unity of all Christians as brothers and sisters. In the words of John Paul II, "The will of Christ impels us to work earnestly and perseveringly for unity with all our Christian brethren...."[32]

We find God's will manifested in each day's events and situations, and in the responsibilities and circumstances of each of our lives. In this regard, the Council says:

> All of Christ's faithful, therefore, whatever be the conditions, duties, and circumstances of their lives, will grow in holiness day by day through these very situations, if they accept all of them with faith from the hand of their heavenly Father, and if they cooperate with the divine will.[33]

Christians must also read the will of God in the "signs of the times." This expression was

The Church's "Yes" to God

frequently used by John XXIII and by the Council to indicate those events in which a Christian, enlightened by faith, can discern God's will in the course of history.

> The People of God believes that it is led by the Spirit of the Lord, who fills the earth. Motivated by this faith, it labors to decipher authentic signs of God's presence and purpose in the happenings, needs, and desires in which this People has a part along with other men of our age. For faith throws a new light on everything, [and] manifests God's design....[34]

We also find God's will expressed in the commands which Jesus has given us.

And lastly, God's will is manifested to us by our superiors. Christians must look upon the words of the bishops as an expression of God's will because the bishops represent Christ. This is underscored by the Council:

> In the bishops...Our Lord Jesus Christ is present in the midst of those who believe.... Bishops in an eminent and visible way undertake Christ's own role as Teacher, Shepherd and High Priest....[35]

Paul VI points out that authority in the Church is not self-constituted but was instituted by Christ who said, "Who hears you hears me" (Lk. 10:16).[36]

And in its decree on the religious life, the Council says:

> Religious, therefore, should be humbly submissive to their superiors, in a spirit of faith and of love for God's will, and in accordance with their rules and constitutions. They should bring their powers of intellect and will and their gifts of nature and grace to bear on the execution of commands and on the fulfillment of the tasks laid upon them.... In this way, far from lowering the dignity of the human person, religious obedience leads it to maturity by extending the freedom of [the children of God].[37]

The saints regard the word of one's spiritual director or confessor as God's will. In the diary of Veronica Giuliani we read:

> Whenever I thought the Lord was commanding me to do something and was saying that this was what he wanted, and that on his behalf I should say this to the one who represented him, I would tell this to my confessors. But they almost always contradicted me.... Nevertheless, this gave me peace, for I felt that I could recognize God's will even more in what my confessor commanded than in what I had received in prayer.[38]

The Church's "Yes" to God 67

LISTEN TO "THAT VOICE"

The compass that indicated God's will to us was "that voice," the voice within us, the voice of the Spirit. For with the coming of Jesus, God has written his law—which is his will—in our human hearts.

Paul exhorts us to "walk by the Spirit" (Gal. 5:16), and he says that "all who are led by the Spirit of God" are children of God (Rom. 8:14).

The Spirit has his own way of speaking to us and he makes his voice heard in our hearts.

At this point, however, we might wonder how non-Christians are able to discern God's will. In this regard, the Second Vatican Council states that, in addition to Divine Revelation, there is another privileged means for perceiving God's will which every person possesses: conscience.

> In the depths of his conscience, man detects a law which he does not impose upon himself, but which holds him to obedience. Always summoning him to love good and avoid evil, the voice of conscience can when necessary speak to his heart more specifically: do this, shun that. For man has in his heart a law written by God...(cf. Rom. 2:14-16).[39]

68 OUR YES TO GOD

Here is what Paul VI says about this voice:

> Is there a duty that exists independently of the obligations deriving from the laws of society? Yes, there is; and it springs from within us: it is the voice of conscience. We all hear it...and it says to us: "You must!..." But this is not simply an innate impulse, a part of our psychological makeup: its source is a higher principle, a transcendent will, which re-echoes within us, interpreting and guiding our being in conformity with the divine mind. For God wants us to be as he conceived us to be, so that we may reach the fullness of our true nature, a nature that is free and progressing, designed to lead us to our fulfillment and to the merging of our lives with his wise and loving plan.[40]

THE PRESENT MOMENT

The Lord taught us to live the present moment in various ways. In the Gospels, for instance, it is evident that we should live the present moment. For we find there that we are to ask the Father for bread only for "this day" (Mt. 6:11); we are told, "Today has troubles enough of its own" (Mt. 6:34*); and we are warned: "No one who puts his hand to the plow and looks back is fit for the kingdom of God" (Lk. 9:62).

The saints, too, encouraged everyone to live the present moment. Catherine of Siena used to say, "The fatigue of the past is no longer ours, because its time has gone; what is to come we do not possess, because we are not sure if its time will ever come."[41]

Another saint who stands out in this regard is the third century abbot, Anthony. One of the principal points in his teachings was: to begin anew "today," in purity of heart and obedience to God's will. This is brought out in his biography, written by Athanasius of Alexandria.

> He himself took no account of the time which had passed, but day by day, as if beginning his ascetical life anew, he made greater efforts to advance, constantly repeating to himself Saint Paul's saying, "I forget the past and I strain ahead for what is still to come" (Phil. 3:13-14). He also recalled the words of the Prophet Elias who said, "As the Lord lives, whom I serve, I shall present myself before him today!" (1 Kings 18:15).[42]

Therese of Lisieux is an expert on how to live the present moment.

> Let us turn our single moment of suffering to profit, let us see each instant as if there were no other. An instant is a treasure....[43]
>
> My life is a flash of lightning, an hour that passes, a moment that fast excapes me and is gone. *My God, you know that to love you on earth I have nothing but today!*[44]

> A moment at a time, you can endure quite a lot.[45]
>
> I'm suffering only for an instant. It's because we think of the past and the future that we become discouraged and fall into despair.[46]
>
> This isn't like persons who suffer from the past or the future; I myself suffer only at each present moment. So it's not any great thing.[47]

Frances Xavier Cabrini wrote this beautiful piece of advice in one of her letters:

> Now what is done is done. Do not live in the past but in the present, and always look ahead to see what virtues you should practice in order to become a saint, a great saint, and soon too.[48]

And the popes are of one mind with the saints. John XXIII lived by the following norm:

> I must do everything, say every prayer, obey the Rule, as if I had nothing else to do, as if the Lord had put me in this world for the sole purpose of doing that thing well, as if my sanctification depended on that alone, without thinking of anything else.[49]

CHAPTER FOUR

*The Church's "Yes" to God
(part two)*

The expressed and unforeseen aspects of God's will

At the beginning of the Movement, as I have mentioned, we saw that some aspects of God's will are clearly expressed—in the Commandments, the words of Jesus, the duties of our state in life, etc.— and that other aspects of his will are unforeseen and are made known to us through circumstances.

Francis de Sales, a great saint and doctor of the Church, describes these two aspects of God's will in his *Treatise on the Love of God*. In book eight of the *Treatise* he explains that we show our adherence to the expressed will of God by being faithful to the Commandments, docile to the evangelical councils and to inspirations, and obedient to the Church and to our superiors.

In book nine he speaks of God's will as it is manifested to us by circumstances, and he says that our conformity to God's will in these instances is shown by our accepting the tribulations that God permits, but even more so by our practice of "holy

OUR YES TO GOD

indifference,"[1] that is, by our being totally available for whatever God may want.

Teresa of Avila manifests this "indifference," or better still, this complete abandonment to God's will, in a poem she wrote, whose refrain is: "What do you wish to do with me?" Here are a few verses:

> I am yours, I was born for you—
> What do you wish to do with me?
>
> Give me life or give me death,
> Give me sickness, give me health,
> Give me strength or make me weak;
> Give me war or perfect peace,
> Revered by all or in disgrace,
> I say my "yes" to all you choose.
> What do you wish to do with me?
>
> Give me wealth or make me poor,
> Give me comfort, leave me sad,
> Give me sorrow, give me joy;
> Give me hell or grant me heaven,
> A sweet life in the sun's pure light—
> For I surrender all to you.
> What do you wish to do with me?
>
> If you wish, permit me to pray,
> If you do not, let me be dry;
> Make me fruitful and devout,
> Or, if you wish, a barren land.
> Sovereign Lord, in your will alone

Can I possess true peace.
What do you wish to do with me?

* * * * *

I am yours, I was born for you—
What do you wish to do with me?[2]

When Augustine speaks of God's will as manifested to us by circumstances God permits, he acknowledges that we must do our best to lessen the annoyance and discomfort which accompany illness and misfortune, and that we may also seek a way out of such situations. But he reiterates that whatever the divine will disposes represents our true good.

> Hence, if anything befalls us contrary to what we pray for, by bearing it patiently, and giving thanks in all things, we should never doubt that we ought to ask what the will of God intends and not what we will ourselves. For our Mediator gave us an example of this when He said, "Father, if it be possible, let this chalice pass from me," then, transforming the human will...He added immediately, "Nevertheless, not as I will but as you will, Father" (Mt. 26:39).[3]
>
> By putting the divine will before his human will, Man rises from the human to the divine.[4]

Of course, all of us constantly aspire to enjoy

peace and health and to be able to work. But what truly counts is God's will. And it is above all by doing his will that we contribute to the progress of the Church.

In every age and in many ways the saints have made clear that, no matter what, God's will is always our greatest good, even if it is painful. Augustine asks, "What does God want from you, or what does he demand of you, if not what is for your good?"[5] And elsewhere he adds:

> The upright of heart are those who in this life follow God's will. The divine will is that at times you should be healthy, at times ill. If, when you are healthy, God's will is pleasant for you, and it is bitter, instead, when you are ill, you are not upright of heart. Why? Because you refuse to conform your will to God's will, but rather you want to bend God's will to fit your own.[6]

GOD'S WILL AND SUFFERING

The saints are so conscious of the value of suffering in this life and they have so often experienced that God "disciplines" and "chastises" those he loves (Heb. 12:6),[7] that in suffering they see nothing but God's will. Teresa of Avila explains it in this way:

> So I want you to realize...what you are giving

The Church's "Yes" to God 77

Him when you pray that His will may be done in you. Do not fear that He will give you riches or pleasure or great honors or any such earthly things; His love for you is not so poor as that!... Would you like to see how He treats those who make this prayer from their hearts? Ask His glorious Son, who made it thus in the Garden. Think with what resolution and fullness of desire He prayed; and consider the manner in which He was answered.

And she then goes on to speak of Jesus' death on the cross and concludes:

So this is what God gave to [the One He loved most], and from that you can understand what His will is.

These, then, are His gifts in this world. He gives them in proportion to the love which He bears us. He gives more to those whom He loves most, and less to those He loves least.[8]

For Paul of the Cross:

Whoever wants to be holy longs to follow in the footsteps of Jesus.... His food is to do in all things the most holy will of God. And since this is done more in suffering than in pleasure, because in pleasure one always becomes attached to one's own will, the true servant of God loves the bare cross, receiving it directly from the most pure will of the Lord.[9]

John Bosco considers obedience and putting up with cold, heat, wind, and all our everyday sufferings as the penance that God offers us to enable us to attain heaven. He tells us of this conversation he had with Dominic Savio:

> Once I found him quite downcast, exclaiming, "Poor me!... The Savior says that if I don't do penance, I won't go to heaven; and I have been forbidden to do penance: so what heaven shall I have?"
> "The penance that the Lord wants from you," I told him, "is obedience. Obey and that is enough for you."
> "Couldn't you allow me some other penance?"
> "Yes, you are allowed the penances of bearing patiently whatever wrongs may be done to you, and of tolerating with resignation the heat, cold, wind, rain, fatigue, and all the discomforts and ailments God may be pleased to send your way."
> "But we have no choice but to suffer these things."
> "By offering to God what you must necessarily suffer, it becomes virtue and gains merit for your soul."[10]

Some further insights into how we ought to act in the midst of suffering are contained in the words of Elizabeth of the Trinity:

> ...everyone who desires to live in communion with Him must imitate His example.... We must

allow ourselves to be immolated by all that the Father wills, after the example of Christ whom we adore.[11]

May his holy will be the sword which immolates you at every moment.[12]

And Josemaría Escrivá de Balaguer writes,

You suffer and you want to bear it in silence. It doesn't matter if you complain—it's the natural reaction of our poor flesh—as long as your will wants, now and always, only what God wants.[13]

ALL THAT GOD WILLS OR PERMITS

The idea that everything that happens is for the best, has been of fundamental importance in the building up of the Movement* that God has entrusted to us. We understood that everything that happened—not only what God willed, but also whatever he permitted—was directed toward our sanctification. Knowing this, we were able to exploit even our mistakes for the kingdom of God.

Once again we were enlighted by the words of

---

*The Focolare Movement is composed of several branches—the Focolarini (consecrated lay people and priests, living a community life), the married Focolarini, the Volunteers, priests, religious, the GEN Movement for youth, the New Families Movement, the New Humanity Movement. Through these branches the Focolare Movement is engaged in a variety of activities.

80   OUR YES TO GOD

Catherine of Siena: "The one who loves perfectly serves faithfully with a living faith, and truly believes that whatever God gives or permits is given only to santify us...."[14]

THE FRUITS OF DOING GOD'S WILL

Let us now consider what the saints say we will experience if we do God's will. Catherine of Siena writes that doing God's will brings peace and tranquility: "Do you want to have peace and tranquility? Then get rid of your will, because every suffering has at its root your own will."[15]

For Josemaria Escrivá de Balaguer, the result of doing God's will is happiness:

> The wholehearted acceptance of the Will of God is the sure way of finding joy and peace: happiness in the Cross. It's then we realize that Christ's yoke is sweet and that His burden is not heavy.[16]
> *So much do I love Your Will, my God, that I wouldn't accept heaven itself against Your Will—if such an absurdity could be.*[17]

In her book *The Foundations,* Teresa of Avila narrates an episode from which we can see that persons who do God's will make great spiritual progress.

Only a few days ago I was speaking with someone who...for almost fifteen years had been kept so busy by obedience [and, therefore, by God's will]...that he could not remember in all that time having had a day to himself.... The Lord rewarded him...because, without realizing [how], he found himself in possession of that precious and very dear freedom of spirit found in [those who are] perfect and in which, truly, one enjoys all the happiness that can be desired in this life. One so favored desires nothing and possesses everything, fears nothing and desires nothing: is not upset by trials, nor exalted by consolations....

The same thing happened...to a number of other persons I know. Some of them I had not seen for years—even for a great many years—and when I asked them what they had been doing, they would say they had spent all their time in occupations imposed upon them by obedience and charity. And yet I found them so far advanced in spiritual matters that I was astounded.[18]

For Vincent de Paul, the result of doing God's will is a continual celebration: "What greater consolation could there be than to do God's will? You who are in the habit of doing it know that it is a continual banquet."[19] He, too, notices considerable spiritual progress in those who persevere in doing God's will.

> Observe...the Christian who has submitted to the Will of God...he can say with the prophet:

"You have held me by my right hand; and by your will you have conducted me..." (Ps. 73:23-24). God holds him, as it were, by the right hand...so that you will see him today, tomorrow, the day after, for a whole week, a whole year and, indeed, during his whole life, living in a state of peace and tranquility.... If you compare him with those who follow their own inclinations you will see all his actions resplendent with light and ever fruitful in results. A noteworthy progress may be observed in his person, a unique force and energy in his works. God gives a special blessing to all he undertakes....[20]

It is striking to see how much this saint insists that union with and abandonment to God's will is the best way, *the* way to holiness.

Very often we are not sure what it means to give glory to God and, consequently, we do not known how to go about it. Listen to what Vincent de Paul has to say:

God is more glorified by the practice of union with His will than by all the other [practices]....[21]

[Doing God's will] gives glory to God by rendering Him that submission which the creature owes its Creator and, in addition, it gives Him joy and pleasure; yes...it gives joy to God and in it He takes delight.... [By doing God's will] you will give joy to God...you will give joy to the angels who rejoice at the glory which God derives from the obedience rendered to His holy Will by a poor creature, and you will give joy to the Saints, who participate in the joy of God.[22]

Paul of the Cross writes:

With regard to any kind of suffering due to aridity, desolation, abandonment, temptations or anything else, the short cut to recovery is true and peaceful resignation to the divine will.[23]
So for medication I will give you the cure-all, which is total submission to God's holy will, accepting everything as coming directly from his loving hand.[24]

And Frances Xavier Cabrini offers this advice:

Begin today to conform yourselves to God's holy will.... Then you will begin to enjoy—even here on this miserable earth—the indescribable happiness the saints possess in heaven. And you will experience a peace, tranquility, and joy that are truly heavenly.[25]

Louise de Marillac finds that even our physical health benefits when we do God's will.

Your health will benefit much from peace and tranquility of spirit, as well as from your completely abandoning all things to divine providence and allowing yourself to be led by love for God's holy will, which is one of the most necessary practices I know of in order to reach perfection.[26]

Teresa of Avila says that if we do God's will we will receive great favors from him that will lead us forward in the mystical life.

> The more resolute we are in soul and the more we show Him by our actions that the words we use with Him are not words of mere politeness, the more and more does our Lord draw us to Himself...and raise us above all petty earthly things, and above ourselves, in order to prepare us to receive great favors from Him, for His rewards for our service will not end with this life. So much does He value this service of ours that we do not know for what more we can ask, while His Majesty never wearies of giving. Not content with having made this soul one with Himself... He begins to cherish it, to reveal secrets to it, to rejoice in its understanding of what it has gained and in the knowledge which it has of all He has yet to give it. He causes it gradually to lose its exterior senses so that nothing may occupy it. This we call rapture. He begins to make such a friend of the soul that not only does He restore its will to it but He gives it His own also. And these two wills will be very compatible, because, seeing that the soul does what He wants, He is glad to allow it to rule with Him. He does what the soul asks of Him.... As we say, the soul will command and He will obey....[27]

Mary and God's Will

From the very beginning of the Movement, we regarded Mary as an outstanding example of what it means to do God's will.

Here is how Augustine explains Mary's true greatness and her true kinship with Jesus:

> When...they told Jesus, who was speaking with his disciples, that his mother and brothers were outside waiting, he replied: "Who is my mother, and who are my brothers?" And stretching out his hand toward his disciples he said, "Here are my mother and my brothers! For whoever does the will of my Father in heaven is my brother, and sister, and mother" (Mt. 12:48-50). Therefore, Mary too was his mother, inasmuch as she did the will of the Father. It is this that the Lord wants to exalt in her: that she has done the Father's will; not that she has generated the flesh of the Word from her flesh....[28]

One person who really loves Mary is Maximilian Kolbe. In one of his letters he writes:

> With no qualms at all you may use the expressions: "I want to carry out the will of Mary Immaculate"; "May the will of Mary Immaculate be done"...because she wants what Jesus wants, and he wants what the Father wants.
>
> Certainly, by referring so unreservedly to her will, you are, by that very fact, declaring that you

86 OUR YES TO GOD

love God's will; and, at the same time, you are witnessing to the truth that her will is so perfect that it does not differ in any way from God's will. And you are glorifying God, Father and Son, for having created such a perfect human being, and for having made her his Mother.[29]

How to do God's Will

When it comes to the question of how to go about doing God's will, Catherine of Siena says that "we must kill our own will—and not halfway, but completely."[30] Paul of the Cross declares: "Whenever we feel some desire arise...to do what, for the moment, is not within our power, we must immediately silence this desire in God's holy will."[31] And he writes the following to a married friend:

> You can best foster your desires to do good by reducing them to one alone, namely, to do in everything the most holy will of God...without neglecting in the slightest way, the obligations of your married state, since this is God's will: that you be perfect in the state of holy matrimony.[32]

John Paul II, speaking to the priests of the United States during his visit in 1979, explained that we must surrender ourselves to God's will:

The Church's "Yes" to God

...the surrender to God's call can be made with utmost confidence and without reservation. Our surrender to God's will must be total—the "yes" given once for all which has as its pattern the "yes" spoken by Jesus Himself. As St. Paul tells us, "...I declare that my word to you is not 'yes' one minute and 'no' the next. Jesus Christ...was not alternatively 'yes' and 'no'; he was never anything but 'yes'" (2 Cor. 1:18-19).[33]

Many of the saints also say that we must abandon ourselves to God's will. Elizabeth of the Trinity, for example, writes: "Yes...let us live for love, always surrendered, immolating ourselves at every moment, by doing God's will without searching for extraordinary things...."[34]

For years now, we have seen how helpful it is—as a way of doing the will of God well—to offer him, one by one, each action of the day, saying: "This is for you." It seemed evident to us that the inspiration to do so had come from the Holy Spirit, particularly in light of the way this practice was enthusiastically received by all the members of the Movement. And now we find this confirmed by one of the saints—Vincent de Paul:

> ...I wish, however, that we accustom ourselves to the practice of offering to God all that we do and suffer, and say to Him: "...I wish it, Lord...."

...How important it is...to accustom oneself to the frequent renewal of this special intention [by saying, "This is for you"], especially in the morning on rising.... Finally, we should aim at raising our hearts to Him in our principal actions, that we may consecrate them to Him entirely and do them in conformity with His Will.

...We shall by this means acquire new titles to love. And love will make us persevere and advance in this holy practice. Practice...is necessary. You must put into practice what I have just told you, if you are to practice the Will of God properly.[35]

The importance of doing God's will

Since the saints realized the importance of doing God's will, they were quick to take advantage of any means that might help them to do so. Louise de Marillac, who founded the Sisters of Charity together with Vincent de Paul, is an example.

> On the feast of St. Sebastian, I felt prompted to give myself to God so that I might do his holy will all my life. And I offered him the inspiration he had given me: that is, to take a vow in this regard, as soon as I received permission.[36]
>
> *Holy will of my God, how reasonable it is that you should be perfectly accomplished! You are the food of the Son of God on earth and therefore you*

are also what sustains my soul which has received its being from God.[37]

This saint, whose life was an outstanding example of Christian charity, made a pact with those who had chosen to live this life with her, that they would always do God's will.

> So that you may conform yourselves to God's holy will in everything, I remind you of the pact we made all together: to never find fault with the conduct of Divine Providence.[38]

Maximilian Kolbe states emphatically that whoever is convinced of the importance of God's will "does not become attached to his work, or to the place where he is, or even to his prayer life, but solely and exclusively to the will of God, to God through Mary Immaculate."[39]

Veronica Giuliani tells how important doing God's will was for her, even in her mystical experiences:

> The Lord showed me two crowns, one of thorns and the other of jewels. It seemed to me that he was inviting me to tell him which of the two I wanted. I longed for the one of thorns; however, I left it up to his holy will. The Lord granted my desire and placed the crown of thorns on my head; and he

offered the crown of jewels to the Blessed Virgin who was also present.

Jesus was standing there holding a lily and a palm branch, and he told me to take one of them. On the lily was written, "Joys and consolations"; on the palm were written these very words, "Victories and battles." ...I desired the palm but I did not have the boldness to ask for it. All I did was to entrust myself to his divine will. He held out the palm to me, but when it was in my hands, it was no longer palm, but became the cross.[40]

Veronica was a member of the Poor Clares, a cloistered Franciscan order. In the twenty-two thousand pages that she wrote out of obedience, over a span of thirty-four years, the declaration of wanting to do God's will comes up hundreds and hundreds of times, even in the most elevated mystical experiences and as a fruit of these.

Francis de Sales advises us not to pay attention to things and events in themselves, but to the fact that they are God's will.

> Do not attach importance to the things you do in themselves, but think only of the honor that is theirs—no matter how insignificant they may be—because they are willed by God....
>
> Seek each day to make yourself more pure of heart. But to possess this purity, you must appraise

and weigh all things on the scale of the sanctuary, which is nothing other than the will of God.[41]

Lower yourself willingly to do those actions which, externally, are less important, when you know that God wants you to, because it doesn't matter whether the actions we perform are great or small, as long as we carry out God's will. Aspire often to the union of your will with that of our Lord.[42]

And John Bosco adds: "Whoever does God's will in small things, is doing something great in God's eyes."[43]

The Curé of Ars has these encouraging words to say, echoing what we have already heard from Teresa of Avila: "Jesus Christ shows he is ready to do our will if we begin to do his."[44] And if anyone says that doing God's will is difficult, Therese of Lisieux responds that God gives us the grace we need to do his will:

Fortunately I didn't ask for suffering. If I had asked for it, I fear I wouldn't have the patience to bear it. Whereas if it is coming directly from God's will, He cannot refuse to give me the patience and the grace necessary to bear it.[45]

Pope John describes his own attitude toward God's will in vivid and effective terms:

> I live only to obey God's slightest commands. I cannot move a hand, a finger or an eye, I cannot look before me or behind, unless God wills it. In his presence I stand upright and motionless, like the lowliest soldier standing to attention before his officer, ready for [anything], even to cast myself into the flames.[46]

In speaking of priestly life, the Council makes a point which is valid for all of us: when we are faced with many things to do, what we must seek to do first is God's will.

> In today's world men have so many obligations to fulfill.... As a result they are sometimes in danger of scattering their energies in many directions.
>
> For their part, priests [anxiously] seek for a way which will enable them to unify their interior lives with their program of external activities.... [They] can truly build up this unity of life by imitating Christ the Lord.... His food was to do the will of Him who sent him to accomplish His work (cf. Jn. 4:34).[47]

Paul VI clarifies another aspect of God's will for us:

> Everything in us that is necessary, compulsory and unchangeable leads us to realize and affirm that this is God's will. One person may be ill,

another poor, still others may find themselves in tribulation and difficult situations. Then we bow our heads and exclaim with conviction: "Everything is disposed by the Lord!" And here a true dialogue with him can begin.[48]

The following splendid passage is also from Pope Paul. It is contained in his "Thoughts on Death."

> And then—finally—an act of good will: which means not looking back anymore, but doing willingly, simply, humbly, and resolutely the duty resulting from the circumstances in which I now find myself because of your will.
> I want to do quickly, perfectly, gladly, all you ask of me now, even if it far surpasses my strength and demands my life—finally, in this last hour.[49]

In a letter of Elizabeth of the Trinity we read:

> ...Our Lord...told us: "My food is to do the will of Him who sent me" (Jn. 4:34).
> Hold fast therefore to the will of this adorable Master, look on every suffering as well as every joy, as coming directly from Him, and then your life will be like a continual communion, for everything will be, as it were, a sacrament which gives you God Himself. And that is perfectly true, for God cannot be divided; His will is His entire being.[50]

94 OUR YES TO GOD

Yes, we must do God's will, and do it well, for all creation does so. Pope Clement of Rome wrote the following in a letter to his fellow Christians at the end of the first century:

> The heavens move at his direction and peacefully obey him. Day and night observe the course he has appointed them without getting in each other's way. The sun and the moon and the choirs of stars roll on harmoniously in their appointed courses at his command, and with never a deviation. By his will and without dissension or altering anything he has decreed the earth becomes fruitful at the proper seasons and brings forth abundant food for men and beasts and every living thing upon it. The unsearchable, abysmal depths and the indescribable regions of the underworld are subject to the same decrees. The basin of the boundless sea is by his arrangement constructed to hold the heaped up waters, so that the sea does not flow beyond the barriers surrounding it, but does just as he bids it.[51]

Therefore, if everything around us does God's will, so too must we. Peter Chrysologus is another who encourages us to do so:

> "His will be done on earth as it is in heaven" (cf. Mt. 6:10). *On earth as it is in heaven:* when everyone will savor and carry out the will of God alone, then everything will be heaven...then all will be in Christ and Christ will be in all. Then all

will be one—indeed, one single [Christ]—when the one Spririt of God lives in all.[52]

DOING GOD'S WILL MAKES US ONE WITH HIM AND ONE ANOTHER

To conclude, I think it would be useful to read a letter that dates back to the beginning of the Movement, to Christmas of 1946: it is our small echo to humanity's "yes" to God.

> Yes! Yes! Yes!—a vigorous, total, determined, creative "yes" to God's will! We want to arrive at the Christmas crib loaded with gifts.
>
> With all the ardor our hearts possess let us say "Yes!" to God's will—always.
>
> Why are we still so imperfect? Why still so many sins? Why aren't we all fused together in a single unity, whose splendid flower would be the fullness of joy and whose fruits would be...works for heaven?
>
> Because we are still doing our own will!
>
> *If we all do the will of God,* we will very soon be that perfect unity that Jesus wants on earth as in heaven!
>
> Little sisters, far and near—all of you urged on by the same splendid idea—let's all gather at midnight Christmas eve, before the Christ Child, and then, recollected in profound prayer, let our hearts cry out "YES!"

I assure you that if we say it with all our heart, with all our mind, with all our strength, *Jesus will live again in us* and we will all be Jesus—Jesus who walks the earth again, doing good.

And isn't this our dream?

If, then, throughout our life, in each present moment, this "yes" is repeated with equal intensity, we will see that what we have so often asked for and so deeply desired as a Christmas gift—*to be Jesus*—will have come true!

I invite you all to do this, because over each one of us, God has placed a magnificent star—his particular will for each of us—and by following it, we will all arrive in heaven united, and we will see following in the wake of our own light, an array of other stars!...

All that remains now is for each of us to heed this invitation and to say or renew our "yes" to God. May his will take root in each of our hearts and remain there always.

APPENDIX

God's Will in Alphonsus Liguori, Doctor of the Church

In the course of this book I never mentioned the teaching of Alphonsus Liguori* regarding God's will, so that I might devote this appendix to his writings on the subject. I will be citing numerous passages from one of his works entitled, quite appropriately, *Uniformity with God's Will.*[1]

The spirituality of Alphonsus is centered on love for God, expressed in concrete terms as the uniting of our will to God's will. Thus, for Alphonsus, as for us, to love God means to do his will

---

*St. Alphonsus Liguori (1696-1787) had already embarked on a successful career as a lawyer when he abandoned law to become a priest. He committed himself to the evangelization of the poorest among the poor. And for this purpose he founded the Redemptorists, who soon became popular as they traveled through towns and villages preaching missions. Alphonsus was made a bishop but he later resigned from this office to dedicate himself to his specific vocation. A renowned theologian, he also wrote many works for the common people on religious topics, and in the process he renewed the theology of his day and contributed to the development of the Italian language. He is particularly venerated because of the apostolic and doctrinal content of this teachings which gave rise to a strong current of renewal in the Church. Many congregations have adopted the rule of St. Alphonsus, adapting it to their own vocation. He is the patron of confessors and moral theologians. His feast day is August 1.

and, consequently, perfection lies entirely in doing God's will.

> Perfection is founded entirely on the love of God: *"Charity is the bond of perfection"* (Col. 3:14), and perfect love of God means the complete union of our will with God's.... Mortification, meditation, receiving Holy Communion, acts of fraternal charity are all certainly pleasing to God—but only when they are in accordance with his will. When they do not accord with God's will, he not only finds no pleasure in them, but he even rejects them utterly and punishes them.[2]

We too have learned that we should do the good that God wants, and that to do the good that God does not want is bad. As Vincent de Paul says, "Good is bad when it is done where God does not want it."[3]

Alphonsus is impressed by how the saints have always done God's will:

> To do God's will—this was the goal upon which the saints constantly fixed their gaze. They were fully persuaded that in this consists the entire perfection of the soul. Blessed Henry Suso used to say: "It is not God's will that we should abound in spiritual delights, but that in all things we should submit to his holy will." ...A certain Dominican nun was granted a vision of heaven one day. She

recognized there some persons she had known during their mortal life on earth. It was told to her that these souls were raised to the sublime heights of the seraphim on account of the uniformity of their wills with that of God's during their lifetime here on earth.[4]

St. Vincent de Paul said, "Conformity with the will of God is the treasure of a Christian and the remedy for all evils, since it comprises self-denial, union with God, and all virtues."...

Some souls given to prayer, upon reading of the ecstasies and raptures of St. Teresa, St. Philip Neri, and other saints, wish that they also might come to enjoy these supernatural unions. Such wishes must be banished.... If we really desire to be saints, we must aspire after true union with God which is to unite our will entirely to the will of God.[5]

According to Alphonsus, life *as it is in heaven* is the norm for our life on this earth:

During our sojourn in this world, we should learn from the saints now in heaven, how to love God. The pure and perfect love of God they enjoy there, consists in uniting themselves perfectly to his will. It would be the greatest delight of the seraphim to pile up sand on the seashore or to pull weeds in a garden for all eternity, if they found out such was God's will. Our Lord himself teaches us to ask to do the will of God on earth as the saints do it in heaven: *"Thy will be done on earth as it is in heaven"* (Mt. 6:10).[6]

Alphonsus further states that "a single act of perfect uniformity with the divine will suffices to make a saint."[7] And he has consoling words for those who think they have little to give to God, little strength to love him because they are sick, and little to give to the poor, and are, therefore, tempted to envy those who are martyrs, missionaries, or heroes:

> He who gives his goods in alms, his blood in scourgings, his food in fasting, gives God what he *has*. But he who gives God his will, gives himself, gives everything he *is*. Such a one can say: "Though I am poor, Lord, I give you all I possess...."[8]

Alphonsus makes a distinction between conformity with the divine will and uniformity with the divine will.

> If we want to be completely pleasing to the heart of God, let us strive in all things to conform ourselves to his divine will. Let us not only strive to conform ourselves, but also to unite ourselves to whatever dispositions God makes of us. *Conformity* signifies that we join our wills to the will of God. *Uniformity* means more—it means that we make one will of God's will and ours, so that we will only what God wills; that God's will alone, is our will.[9]

God's Will in Alphonsus Liguori 103

Sometimes we are troubled by the things that happen to us or around us, because we do not know whether what is happening is God's will. But listen to what Alphonsus says:

> ...It is certain and of faith, that whatever happens, happens by the will of God.... And our Lord himself told St. Peter that his sacred passion came not so much from man as from his Father: *"Shall I not drink the cup which the Father has given me?"* (Jn. 18:11)
>
> When the messenger came to announce to Job that the Sabeans had plundered his goods and slain his children, he said: *"The Lord gave and the Lord has taken away"* (Job 1:21). He did not say "The Lord has given me my children and my possessions, and the Sabeans have taken them away."[10]

And those who live according to this conviction are greatly blessed by God:

> Cesarius points up what we have been saying by offering this incident in the life of a certain monk: Externally his religious observance was the same as that of the other monks, but he had attained such sanctity that the mere touch of his garments healed the sick. Marveling at these deeds, since his life was no more exemplary than the lives of the other monks, the superior asked him one day what was the cause of these miracles.

He replied that he too was mystified and was at a loss as to how to account for such happenings. "What devotions do you practice?" asked the abbot. He answered that there was little or nothing special that he did beyond making a great deal of willing only what God willed, and that God had given him the grace of abandoning his will totally to the will of God.

"Prosperity does not lift me up, nor adversity cast me down," added the monk. "I direct all my prayers to the end that God's will may be done fully in me and by me." "That raid that our enemies made against the monastery the other day, in which our stores were plundered, our granaries put to the torch and our cattle driven off—did not this misfortune cause you any resentment?" queried the abbot.

"No, Father," came the reply. "On the contrary, I returned thanks to God—as is my custom in such circumstances—fully persuaded that God does all things, or permits all that happens, for his glory and for our greater good; thus I am always at peace, no matter what happens." Seeing such uniformity with the will of God, the abbot no longer wondered why the monk worked so many miracles.[11]

Alphonsus considers that everything that happens is for the best.

God's Will in Alphonsus Liguori 105

God wills only our good; God loves us more than anybody else can or does love us.... Even chastisements come to us, not to crush us, but to make us mend our ways and save our souls: *"Let us believe that these scourges of the Lord have happened for our amendment and not for our destruction"* (Judith 8:27).[12]

When persons make God's will their own, God frequently does what they want. "Indeed," says Alphonsus, "what can be more satisfactory to a person than to experience the fulfillment of all his desires? This is the happy lot of the man who wills only what God wills...."[13]

Alphonsus observes that a person who does God's will is always consistent:

The Holy Spirit warns us: *"Do not winnow with every wind"* (Sir. 5:11), that is: "Do not be swayed by every wind that blows." Some people resemble weather vanes that turn about according to which way the wind blows. If the wind is favorable to their desires, you see them cheerful and good-natured; but if there is a contrary wind and things do not turn out as they wish, you see them sad and impatient. And so they do not become saints and they lead an unhappy life....[14]

Alphonsus assures us that the fruit of uniformity with God's will is a foretaste of heaven.

> By uniting themselves to the divine will, the saints have enjoyed paradise by anticipation in this life.... St. Mary Magdalene of Pazzi derived such consolation at hearing the words "will of God," that she usually fell into an ecstasy of love.[15]

Like the other saints, Alphonsus invites us to pray in order that we may accomplish God's will:

> When anything disagreeable happens, remember it comes from God and say at once, "This comes from God" and be at peace.... Form the habit of offering yourself frequently to God by saying, "My God, behold me in your presence; do with me and all that I have as you please." This was the constant practice of St. Teresa. At least fifty times a day she offered herself to God, placing herself at his entire disposition and good pleasure.[16]
>
> St. Mary Magdalene of Pazzi used to say that all our prayers should have no other purpose than that of obtaining from God the grace to follow his holy will in all things.[17]

He then explains in great detail those matters in which we should unite ourselves to God's will:

God's Will in Alphonsus Liguori 107

In external matters. In times of great heat, cold or rain; in times of famine, epidemics and similar occasions we should refrain from expressions like these: "What unbearable heat!" "What piercing cold!" "What a tragedy!" In these instances we should avoid expressions indicating opposition to God's will....

In personal matters. In matters that affect us personally, let us acquiesce in God's will. For example, in hunger, thirst, poverty, desolation, loss of reputation....

Let us not lament if we suffer from some *natural defect* of body or mind; from poor memory, slowness of understanding, little ability...or general bad health....

Who knows? Perhaps if God had given us greater talent, better health, a more personable appearance, we might have lost our souls!...

It is especially necessary that we be resigned in *corporal infirmities*.... We ought to make use of the ordinary remedies...but if they are not effective, let us unite ourselves to God's will and this will be better for us than would be our restoration to health.... Certainly, it is more virtuous not to complain in times of painful illness; still and all, when our sufferings are excessive, it is not wrong to let our friends know what we are enduring, and also to ask God to free us from our sufferings.... We have the example of our Lord, who, at the approach of his bitter passion, made known his state of soul to his disciples, saying: *"My soul is sorrowful even unto death"* (Mt. 26:38) and besought his eternal Father to deliver him from it.... But our Lord likewise taught us what we should do when we have made such a petition, when he added: *"Nevertheless, not as I will, but as you will"* (Mt. 26:39).[18]

The time of spiritual desolation is also a time for being resigned. When a soul begins to cultivate the spiritual life, God usually showers his consolations upon it...but when he sees it making solid progress, he withdraws his hand to test its love.... I do not say you will feel no pain in seeing yourself deprived of the sensible presence of God; it is impossible for the soul not to feel it and lament over it, when even our Lord cried out on the cross: *"My God, my God, why have you forsaken me?"* (Mt. 27:46). In its sufferings, however, the soul should always be resigned to God's will.[19]

Finally, we should be united to God's will in regard to the *time* and *manner* of our death. One day St. Gertrude, while climbing up a small hill, lost her footing and fell into a ravine below. After her companions had come to her assistance, they asked her if while falling she had any fear of dying without the sacraments. "I earnestly hope and desire to have the benefit of the sacraments when death is at hand," she replied; "still, to my way of thinking, the will of God is more important...."[20]

Lastly, we should unite ourselves to the will of God as regards our *degree* of grace and glory....

God's Will in Alphonsus Liguori 109

We should desire to love God more than the seraphim, but not to a degree higher than God has destined for us.[21]

Last but not least, Alphonsus stresses the importance of doing God's will as it is expressed for us by our superiors:

St. Vincent de Paul used to say, "God is more pleased by the sacrifice we offer him when we subject our will to obedience, than by all the other sacrifices we can offer him; because in giving him other things...we give him things we possess, but in giving him our will we give him ourselves."[22]

Notes

Chapter 1

1. Claus Westermann, *Genesis,* 1. Teilband: "Genesis 1-11," in *Biblischer Kommentar, Altes Testament* (Neukirchen, 1974), Vol. 1, p. 218.

Chapter 2

1. See the section devoted to this same topic in Chapter 3.
2. See Ephesians 4:22-24.
3. Francis de Sales, *Treatise on the Love of God,* VIII, 7, trans. Henry Mackey, O.S.B. (Westminster, Md.: The Newman Bookshop, 1945), pp. 340-341.
4. Catherine of Siena, Letter 5, in *Epistolario* (Alba, 1966), Vol. 2, p. 220.

Chapter 3

1. Maria Winowska, *The Death Camp Proved Him Real,* trans. Therese Plumereau (Kenosha: Prow Books, 1971), p. 31.
2. *Treatise on the Love of God,* VIII, 7, p. 340.
3. J.M. Perrin, O.P., *Catherine of Siena,* trans. Paul Barrett, O.F.M. Cap. (Westminster, Md.: Newman Press, 1965), p. 142.
4. Perrin, *Catherine of Siena,* p. 143.
5. Letter 132, in *Epistolario,* II, p. 489.
6. Teresa of Avila, *The Interior Castle,* II, 8, in *The Complete Works of St. Teresa of Avila,* trans. and ed. E. Allison Peers (New York: Sheed & Ward, 1950), Vol. 2, p. 301.
7. *The Foundations,* V, 10, in *The Complete Works,* Vol. 3, p. 23.
8. *Spiritual Relations,* XIX, in *The Complete Works,* Vol. 1, p. 344.
9. Paul of the Cross, Letter 162, *Letters of St. Paul of the Cross,* trans. by Passionist Fathers (Manuscript in Immaculate Conception Monastery Library, Jamaica, N.Y.), p. 162.
10. Paul VI to the general audience, June 14, 1972 *The Teachings of Pope Paul VI: 1972* (Washington, D.C.: USCC, 1973), pp. 83-84.
11. John XXIII, *Journal of a Soul,* trans. Dorothy White (New York: McGraw-Hill, 1965), p. 112.
12. Paul VI, Address on the feast of St. Joseph (March 19, 1968), *Insegnamenti di Paolo VI,* VI (Rome: Poliglotta Vaticana, 1969), pp. 1154-1155.

13. Josemaría Escrivá de Balaguer, *The Way* (New York: Scepter, 1979), p. 176.
14. *The Way*, p. 179.
15. *Lettere di San Paolo della Croce,* ed. Padre Amedeo della Madre del Buon Pastore (Rome, 1924), Vol. 1, p. 491.
16. John of the Cross, *The Ascent of Mount Carmel,* 21, 4, in *The Collected Works of St. John of the Cross,* trans. K. Kavanaugh and O. Rodriguez (Washington, D.C.: ICS Publications, 1973), Vol. 2, p. 174.
17. Sr. Elizabeth of the Trinity, Letter 169, *J'ai trouvé Dieu,* Ib (Paris: Ed. du Cerf, 1980), p. 168.
18. General audience, March 12, 1969, *Teachings: 1969* (1970), p. 50.
19. General audience, August 25, 1971, *Teachings: 1971* (1972), p. 131.
20. Augustine, *Enarr. in Ps. (On the Psalms),* XXXII, 2, s.1, 2.
21. L. DiPinto, *Volontà del Padre,* in N.D.S. (Rome: Ed. Paoline, 1979), p. 1715.
22. *The Ascent of Mount Carmel,* II, 22, 3, in *The Collected Works,* p. 179.
23. Cyprian, *De dominica oratione (Treatise on the Lord's Prayer),* XV.
24. *St. Therese of Lisieux, Her Last Conversations,* trans. John Clarke, O.C.D. (Washington, D.C.: ICS, 1977), p. 63.
25. St. Therese of Lisieux, *Story of a Soul,* trans. John Clarke, O.C.D. (Washington, D.C.: ICS, 1975), p. 27. (Italics ours).

26. *Last Conversations,* pp. 97-98.
27. St. Therese of Lisieux, *J'entre dans la vie* (Paris: Cerf-DDB, 1973), p. 235.
28. *Thoughts of Soeur Therese of the Child Jesus* (New York, 1915), p. 117.
29. *Declaration on Religious Freedom,* 14, in *The Documents of Vatican II,* ed. W.M. Abbott and J. Gallagher (New York: America Press, 1966), p. 694. Unless otherwise noted, all Council quotes are taken from the edition here cited, and are used with permission of America Press, Inc., 106 W. 56th Street, New York, N.Y. 10019 © 1966 All Rights Reserved.
30. *Dogmatic Constitution on the Church,* 13, in *The Documents,* p. 30.
31. *Pastoral Constitution on the Church in the Modern World,* 93, in *The Documents,* p. 307.
32. John Paul II to the American Bishops, October 5, 1979, *U.S.A.—The Message of Justice, Peace and Love* (Boston: St. Paul Editions, 1979), p. 187.
33. *The Church,* 41, in *The Documents,* p. 70.
34. *The Church in the Modern World,* 11, in *The Documents,* p. 209.
35. *The Church,* 21, in *The Documents,* pp. 41-42.
36. See *Insegnamenti di Paolo VI,* II (Rome: Poligiotta Vaticana, 1965), p. 980.
37. *Decree on the Renewal of the Religious Life,* 14, in *Vatican II, The Conciliar and Post Conciliar Documents,* ed. Austin Flannery, O.P. (Wilmington, 1975), p. 619.

38. Veronica Giuliani, *Il mio calvario,* ed. P. Pizzicaria (Città di Castello, 1960), p. 126.
39. *The Church in the Modern World,* 16, in *The Documents,* p. 213.
40. General audience, August 9, 1972, *Insegnamenti di Paolo VI,* X (1973), pp. 797-798.
41. Letter 151, *Epistolario,* II, p. 97.
42. St. Athanasius, *The Life of St. Anthony,* in *The Fathers of the Church, A New Translation,* ed. R. Deferrari (New York, 1952), Vol. 15.
43. *The Collected Letters of Therese of Lisieux,* ed. Abbé Combes, trans. F.J. Sheed (New York: Sheed & Ward, 1949), p. 102.
44. Therese of Lisieux, *Gli Scritti* (Rome, 1979), p. 818.
45. *J'entre dans la vie,* p. 48.
46. *Last Conversations,* p. 155.
47. *Last Conversations,* p. 241.
48. *The Letters of St. Frances Xavier Cabrini,* trans. Sr. Ursula Infante, M.S.C. (New York, 1969), p. 8.
49. *Journal of a Soul,* p. 98.

CHAPTER 4

1. St. Francis de Sales, *Treatise on the Love of God,* IX, 4, II (Garden City, 1963), p. 105.
2. Teresa of Avila, "Poesias," II, *Obras Completas,* 3rd Ed. (Madrid: Editorial Plenitud, 1964), pp. 935-937.
3. Augustine, Letter 130, *Letters,* Vol. 2, in *The Fa-*

thers of the Church, A New Translation, ed. R. Deferrari (New York, 1953), p. 397.
4. Augustine, *Tractatus in Johannis Evangelium (Homilies on the Gospel of John),* 25, 3.
5. Augustine, *Enarr. in Ps. (On the Psalms),* XXXVI, 2, 13.
6. *Enarr. in Ps.,* XXXV, 16.
7. See Prov. 3:11-12; Job 5:17; Rev. 3:19.
8. *The Interior Castle,* XXXII, 6-7, in *The Complete Works,* Vol. 2, pp. 136–137.
9. *Lettere,* Vol. 1, pp. 616–617.
10. John Bosco, *Scritti Spirituali,* ed. J. Aubry (Rome, 1976), Vol. 1, p. 151.
11. "Retreat: How to find heaven on earth," in *Sr. Elizabeth of the Trinity, Spiritual Writings,* trans. M.M. Philipon, O.P. (London: Geoffrey Chapman, 1962), p. 143.
12. "Letter to Louise Desmoulin," in *Spiritual Writings,* p. 107.
13. *The Way,* p. 168.
14. "Letter to Sano di Marco and others" (62), in Perrin, *Catherine of Siena,* p. 146.
15. Letter 75, in *Il messaggio di Santa Caterina da Siena, dottore della Chiesa,* ed. un missionario vincenziano (Rome, 1970), p. 717.
16. *The Way,* p. 177.
17. *The Way,* p. 178. (Italics ours).
18. *The Foundations,* V, 7-8, in *The Complete Works,* Vol. 3, pp. 21–22.
19. Conference 90, in *The Conferences of St. Vincent de Paul to the Daughters of Charity,* trans. Joseph

Leonard, C.M. (Westminster, Md.: Newman Press, 1952), Vol. 4, p. 54.
20. Conference 24, in *Conferences of St. Vincent de Paul,* ed. Pierre Coste, C.M., trans. Joseph Leonard, C.M. (Philadelphia, 1963), p. 52.
21. Conference 199, in Coste, *Conferences,* p. 490.
22. Conference 48, in *Conferences to the Daughters of Charity,* p. 175.
23. *Lettere,* Vol. 2, p. 264.
24. *Lettere di san Paolo della Croce,* ed. C. Chiari (Rome, 1977), Vol. 5, p. 191.
25. Letter 260, in *Lettere di santa Francesca Saverio Cabrini* (Milan, 1968), p. 563.
26. Letter 643, in *Sainte Louise de Marillac, Ses Ecrits* (Paris, 1961), p. 775.
27. *The Way of Perfection,* XXXII, 12, in *The Complete Works,* Vol. 2, pp. 138-139.
28. *Tractatus in Johannis Evangelium (Homilies on the Gospel of John),* 10, 3.
29. G. Domanski, "Il pensiero mariano di p. Massimiliano Kolbe," *Quaderni della Milizia dell'Immacolata,* Vol. 4 (1971), p. 79.
30. Letter 340, in *Il messaggio,* p. 714.
31. *Lettere di san Paolo della Croce,* ed. p. Amedeo, Vol. 1, p. 49.
32. *Lettere,* ed. p. Amedeo, Vol. 1, p. 611.
33. *U.S.A.—The Message of Justice, Peace and Love,* p. 137.
34. *Spiritual Writings,* p. 102.
35. Conference 199, in Coste, *Conferences,* pp. 497-498.
36. *Ses Ecrits,* p. 895.

37. *Ses Ecrits,* p. 896.
38. Letter 144, in *Ses Ecrits,* p. 190.
39. Maximilian Kolbe, "Scritti," in *Solo l'amore crea,* ed. G. Barra (Turin, 1972), p. 49.
40. *Il mio calvario,* p. 196.
41. Francis de Sales, *Tutte le lettere* (Rome, 1967), Vol. 1, p. 662.
42. *Tutte le lettere,* p. 789.
43. *Scritti spirituali,* Vol. 2, p. 111.
44. The Curé of Ars, *Scritti scelti,* ed. Gérard Rossé (Rome: Città Nuova, 1975), p. 76.
45. *Last Conversations,* p. 290.
46. *Journal of a Soul,* p. 84.
47. *Decree on the Ministry and Life of Priests,* 14, in *The Documents,* p. 562.
48. *Insegnamenti di Paolo VI,* VI (1969), p. 1155.
49. Paul VI, "Pensiero alla morte," *Osservatore Romano,* 5 August 1979, p. 5.
50. *Spiritual Writings,* p. 102.
51. Clement of Rome, "First Letter," 20, in *Early Christian Fathers,* ed. and trans. Cyril C. Richardson (New York: Macmillan, 1970), p. 53.
52. Peter Chrysologus, *Sermones (Sermons),* 72.

APPENDIX

1. Alphonsus de Liguori, *Uniformity with God's Will,* trans. Thomas W. Tobin, C.SS.R., copyright © 1952. Reprinted with permission of the Redemptor-

ist Fathers, Brooklyn, N.Y. The following references all refer to this work unless otherwise indicated.
2. p. 4.
3. Vincent de Paul, Letter 3008, in *Correspondance, Entretiens, Documents,* ed. Pierre Coste, C.M. (Paris, 1923), Vol. 8, p. 151.
4. pp. 5-6.
5. Alphonsus Liguori, *Pratica di amare Gesù Cristo* (Rome, 1973), pp. 173-174.
6. p. 6.
7. p. 6.
8. p. 7.
9. p. 7.
10. pp. 8-9.
11. pp. 9-10.
12. pp. 14-15.
13. p. 11.
14. *Pratica di amare Gesù Cristo,* pp. 175-180.
15. p. 12.
16. p. 16.
17. *Pratica di amare Gesù Cristo,* p. 181.
18. pp. 17-19.
19. pp. 23-24.
20. pp. 26-27.
21. pp. 28-29.
22. Alphonsus Liguori, *Affetti divoti a Gesù Cristo,* in *Opere ascetiche* (Rome, 1933), Vol. 1, pp. 384-385.